THE LITTLEST ENVOY

What a small Schnauzer taught me about humanity

DAVID DAY

Dogs' lives are too short. Their only fault, really.

Agnes Turnbull

For Charlie Gonzalez - Schnauzer, Pedigreed -
Born 2012

Contents

ONE

A Bullet in the Heart

One should know that earnestly loving a dog will probably lead to profound heartbreak. One can also know, it will be worth it.

As an adult, I have had in my household (and lost) three beloved dogs over time. One was lost to accident and two to old age. The experiences led to a promise to myself to simply cherish the most wonderful times and never have to love my way through the full life cycle of another K-9 friend.

Oh, and I did, as a child, have one magnificent dog for

two days. At the age of eleven, I was the only child still left at home. I decided, and quickly convinced my mother, that a dog could keep me from getting too lonely. "Surely," I thought. "for substantive presence and protection, it would be perfect to have an English Bulldog."

"And exactly how much responsibility for caring for this new dog will your mom and I have to shoulder?" My dad asked this before making mean faces that abruptly shut down the whole conversation.

Throwing a comic book in the air, I mustered all the drama that I so loved (even at eleven), screamed, "Okay, I guess I will just die of loneliness in my bedroom and nobody cares," then ran to my room and flung myself on the bed.

Except for my attempt at punishing my father with silence and a pouty face at breakfast the next morning, nothing more came of the conversation.

Nothing more came of the discussion that is, until I walked sleepily and pajama-clad into the living room on Christmas morning.

Seated there under the Christmas tree was the most strikingly perfect English Bulldog puppy anyone could ever find.

He was white with brown spots, a pink nose and huge paws that looked almost too large for his legs to carry. With a big tongue flopping, he ran into my arms. All my life I had wanted a dog, and here was a dream come true in an oversized and pedigreed package. I cried. Mom cried.

I was delighted, my mother was delighted, my father mustered the happiness that Christmas demanded, but still seemed unsure about the development. He never had a dog as a child or as an adult. "It was because of the Great Depression," he said.

What a wonderful Christmas!

I named the dog "Bullet" after Roy Roger's dog, and he was perfect. We played ball. We rolled in the yard. We took a snuggled-up nap. I looked at him and instantly loved him. It was rapture!

When midnight arrived, and all of Santa's little elves were resting; while happy, kids were soundly sleeping with their new toys all over town, there came a strange sound in our house. It was a slapping, rattling sound.

Bullet was snoring. Big, floppy cheeks rose, filled with air, then slapped against his jaw with every breath. His nose then trumpeted in a high-pitched sound when he sucked air back in.

I thought it was hilarious, an opinion shared by no one else in the household. I was awake. Mom was awake. Worse still, dad was awake and clearly declaring he was not happy!

The only one still asleep was Bullet, who droned on with his little one-dog band, sleeping off the puppy excitement of the day.

The next morning brought a family meeting.

"Son," said dad, "we have to do something about that dog."

"But dad," I whiningly protested, "he is just a puppy. It'll get better, I'm sure."

"No son, he will only get bigger and it will only get worse."

"Honey, it's a Christmas present, dream come true," mom protested from across the kitchen.

It became clear dad had been thinking about this during his awakened hours overnight.

"I'll tell you what son," he said. "You let us return the dog, and I'll buy you that department store tape recorder you have been begging for over the past two years."

Apparently now desperate, he had pulled out the big guns for negotiation. That recorder costs almost a hundred dollars. I had longed to have it to help me fulfill my big-picture dream of practicing to be a radio announcer. I had long ago accepted the reality we were poor and I would probably never have an almost one hundred dollar item from the department store.

This was like a bomb; the dog, or the tape recorder! I teared up.

"Whoa, this is just cruel," mom's voice was becoming loud and serious.

Dad furrowed his brow and got that bloated red look on his face that signaled that if he was crossed or pushed one step further, he would explode into a tirade.

"By God, I have to work. I am the only damn one working to support this family. I will not try to get up at five in the morning and drag my ass to work after being awake listening to that percussion section of a dog flopping its cheeks all night! He can have the tape recorder for Christmas or not, but in any case, that dog is going back to where we got it."

I ran outside and sat on the porch sobbing. Breaking a child's spirit is a progressive process punctuated by little moments of squeezing the heart until it almost bursts.

Over time, the spirit becomes so bruised that even the smallest items or gestures can be embraced as escape zones and hiding places. Mine became a tape recorder from the department store.

I simply buried myself in "practicing" being a radio announcer and nursed a hole in my soul where a dog needed to be.

TWO

Destiny is a Mighty Wind

Now as an adult and, after having (for the fourth time in my life) befriended and lost a dog, I decided it could never be allowed to happen again. No more dogs!

A relative who had recently lost a dog was looking for another. Listed on social media, my partner found a lovely little middle-aged Schnauzer female. I held forth as a Schnauzer expert.

"You know, you don't want a male. They are too active and flighty, too much terrier character. Black females are the smartest, most responsible and loving dog you can find. The black ones generally have soft, instead of wiry fur."

The relative seemed convinced. Only problem was that the dog was seventy five miles from our house and a hundred and fifty miles from hers. After a negotiation to buy and adopt the dog, my partner and I agreed to pick it up (on what turned out to be the fourth of July) and keep it at our house until the relative could come get it a few days later.

Traffic was stop-and-go. What should have been an

hour-and-a-half trip, turned out to be an almost three-hour grueling journey.

No one could have expected the scene we found. When the father opened the front door, there appeared a staircase running up to the left where three little children's faces poked through the banisters to anxiously see who had come to get their pet. A fourth, younger child stood in the living room.

The father stood at the front door. There was no dog in sight.

The mother greeted us graciously and smilingly. Clearly picking up on the soulful looks of the kids and our subdued response, she quickly explained that due to family circumstances the dog had to go and that disposition of the matter was on a limited time schedule.

The girl dog, who the children had named "Charlie" after a television character, had been through her own ordeals that apparently had tracked along with some concurrent ordeals in the family.

She had one set of six puppies that had been sold and

taken from her. When it came time to birth a second litter of eight, they breached. After twelve hours of labor, a vet would not deliver the pups unless the family agreed to perform extensive surgery including ovariohysterectomy. Three of the pups survived the surgery, but could not be nurtured by the mother and also died. Charlie, lost a second set of children. She came home accompanied by a huge vet bill and a long recovery.

In addition, she had a stubborn and recurring skin condition that resulted in frequent outbreaks.

With the sad looks of the children and the medical rundown, we started to have some hesitation suggesting this might not work out (despite our three-hour drive).

Then, however, Charlie came on the scene. A door opened and a little black, furry swirl exploded into the room. Without a sound, she first headed straight for my companion, then to me. She was bubbling with excitement. Her generously proportioned ears stuck straight up and she peered out of a beautifully fuzzy black face with huge beckoning eyes.

The whites of her eyes showed just enough at the bottom to amplify the cuteness by about a hundred fold.

The mother pulled Charlie to her own knees, put a hand on each side of the little doggie face and looked at her intently.

"I can tell you right now, those eyes can look right into your soul," she said quietly. Then she reluctantly, but purposefully released Charlie to continue her run from person to person.

Charlie jumped into my lap and then into my arms. We exchanged money and niceties with the mom and I think everyone was crying a little when we started to leave. "She will be perfect for our friend," I told the family. I tried not to look at the kids, but couldn't help myself. Little teary eyes followed us as we walked out the door.

As the door closed, I caught a quick memory of a boy, a Christmas and a bulldog and tears started flooding down my cheeks. I wondered what these kids' tape recorder offer had been.

Now, I climbed into the passenger side so I could hold the dog and wondered what Charlie's reaction would be. She took one quick look out the window at the house, then curled up in my lap, where she slept all the seventy five miles to her new temporary home.

THREE

Attached!

_____

When we got home, Charlie shook herself, looked around and began to explore. If there were any anxiety, it didn't show. She seemed to become buoyed and happy when we fed her right away after the arrival.

Seemingly relaxed, she followed a whole-house exploration with sprawling out chin-down on the rug in the entry where she had a view of both the kitchen and the living room. From there she curiously watched these new people who had just hauled her seventy five miles away from her home.

She had seen a score of her puppy children taken from her side. Now, she was the one who had been taken away. One can't even imagine the meaning to her.

The only hint there was of missing her family was a little searching from room to room, and a little whimpering that night as she slept.

She was beautiful!

With a coat that was very soft and silky for a Schnauzer, she was black with sleek wavy hair and just a few little white fur spots on one back foot. She didn't have the typical clipped Schnauzer ears, but sported instead a wondrous set of four-inch winglike protrusions that could fold, or turn, stick straight up or hang down draped over each side of her face in an endlessly changing display of positioning and emotion.

Ears that could signal a hundred different emotions

We eventually learned that these ears carried a code. Like signal flags in the hands of a sailor, they could convey a score of different messages. Those might include emotions, intentions and circumstances. When first we met, however, they were just very, very cute.

In the morning, she stretched and nuzzled and frolicked. Standing at the door Charlie clearly declared by silently looking over her shoulder that she needed outside. Next, she was politely insistent that she expected breakfast.

I started to put on my socks. Charlie looked me right in the face, grabbed one and burst out of the room. In a frenzy, she ran full blast from room to room, looking over her shoulder at times and enticing me to chase her. From living room to dining room, to kitchen and back she ran. A little black blur raced from chair to couch to floor to the next room, clearly delighted by my chasing behind. Finally stopping on the sofa with the sock dangling in her mouth, she invited the capture by making eye contact.

My grabbing back the sock came amid a flurry of wiggles and snuggles and kisses. Deciding she must have learned this from the kids who raised her, we came to call this "Charlie's Sock Game" and it was a game she would play on occasion until she got too old to run with such abandon.

All too soon on this day two, I became aware that the clock was ticking. "She is going to yet another new home," I told myself. "Don't get attached and don't let her get too attached."

I vowed to stay at arms-length, but it became more and more impossible. This was a pack animal, and she was bent on pack making. She had a combination of a mom, a herder and a guardian set of instincts that kicked in as if she had just taken on new employment. Serious and systematic, she made it clear there was a rhythm to her life and she would let us know what it was. Ultimately, she would be the timekeeper for our days.

Like only one of the previous dogs of her kind I had known, Charlie had what I refer to as "the Schnauzer grunt." This being a soft, low pitched, guttural sound emanating from the chest and quietly signaling approval, or concern, or just a need for attention.

It was generally one, or two, or three quick sounds delivered in a quiet, subtle guttural way and often with direct eye contact. It's a rare soul-based sound that may be easy to miss, but once you hear it, you will never forget.

Charlie's grunts were sometimes paired with stretching out her body and tapping her right paw on the floor a same number of times coordinated with the grunt sequence. The paw taps could be independent or the grunt made separately, but it was particularly emphatic when they came together.

Another unique manner of expression came when she woke up in the morning. She would softly put her paw on one's arm or face and emit a high-pitched-cartoon- character-like yawn sound that was enormously endearing and elicited an immediate hug.

Mostly, she didn't bark. She didn't beg. She was perfectly house trained and exquisitely well mannered. Beyond everything else, she was a lover.

Whether it was softly touching one's leg with her paw to get attention, nudging her nose under one's hand and pitching it upward to get petting to resume, or sprawling out on the couch and pressing her back as tight as she could get it against one's leg, this dog exuded sweet affection.

Then there was the look. She had the most wise and gentle eyes, and when they locked on, they conveyed a huge dose of knowing soul power that was almost hypnotizing.

I was falling in love with a pup, but I kept having to remind myself that my partner's mother was the one who was scheduled to be the ultimate recipient of Charlie.

It was late afternoon on day two, and my partner was running errands when he called me on the phone. "I've been thinking," he opened the conversation.

"I may know the subject," I responded. The exchange then went like this:

"Yeah, ya think?"

"umm hmm," I said, "is this about Charlie?"

"Maybe. Are you sure we want to let her go tomorrow?"

"I thought we weren't going to have any more dogs."

"We're not talking about dogs; we're talking about Charlie."

"Yeah, well, in answer to your question, I'm not ready to let her go tomorrow or ever. Now, I don't want to jerk her up out of this home and make her go to another one. What do we do about your mom?"

"Actually, I hadn't told you, but she wasn't too excited about having a black dog anyway," came the reply.

"Oh, now you tell me!"

"No she kind of wanted a grey Schnauzer. I had to talk her into taking Charlie. She won't mind."

Charlie, in those few sentences, got her new and forever home.

FOUR

Self-Awareness

People talk about how their dogs think they are people. That was never the case with Charlie. She seemed to always know she was a dog, and watching that gave me some profound lessons in self-awareness.

The first hint of all of this came when I noticed she was on the patio and seemed to be peering into the living room through a sliding glass door. Then, I realized the curtains were closed. She was thoughtfully looking for a very long time at her reflection in the window.

She always got excited when she saw other dogs and clearly knew what that looked like. She also certainly recognized individual people. It was very obvious that Charlie had to know she was a dog.

It became quite clear to us quite soon that this creature had a distinct personhood. She declared it in hundreds of ways.

Dogs are unique in their place in the world. We snatch them from their mothers when they are still little babies. They are often not allowed to have the inter-generational wisdom, maternal-imparted instincts or parental instruction that other animals may receive.

They are deprived of the impartation of their native language, but instead, are often forced to make up their own individual sounds to which only they individually can assign meaning (or hope that their humans can decipher some meaning from it).

Emerging research continues to confirm that animals have variable capacity for generational learning. From tool-making among apes, to complex messaging taught to their offspring by whales, animals maintain an evolving inter-generational sharing of vast knowledge.[1] For the most part, we as humans have deprived pet dogs of this.

Many animals have a chance to teach skills to their young

Are we smarter than animals? Scientific evidence is

increasingly showing that we are simply differently smart. Unfortunately, the dog species in general has constant disruption of its ability to share intergenerational intelligence because of purloined puppies.

Where a pack in the wild might have generational pack language and audible signaling passed down, dogs who meet at the doggy park really have no basis for a shared oral language.

When they sometimes see other dogs, they are mixed by breed, language and experience and often don't even bond with those of their own kind. When bonding does occur, they may be ripped from each other at the whims of surrounding humans.

Instead of having a dog world, they are forced into the life of alien beings who hold them captive while fawning over them. Their delicate sensing and balancing whiskers may be sheared, their tails removed in an act of puppy mutilation. Their astounding sense of vision by smell is often obscured by stinky human environments. They are in so many ways reduced and subdued.

What must one of these little animals think of creatures for whom the light comes on when they walk in the room? Maybe they think, "These are beings who can create food from nothing by opening a big silver box. This breed controls huge mechanisms and makes astounding things appear."

Now under the control of these ominous bipeds, and deprived of the ability to access the glorious, wild and regal inheritance of their breed, dogs are relegated to priorities that include the vital requirements of not peeing on the carpet and performing silly routines for food.

They are collared and harnessed and haltered and chained. They are branded with clanging metal tags. Humans feel free to put their fingers in their ears, down their throat and up their ass for whatever reasons at whatever time.

Strangely (and probably because for most of these creatures it is all they have ever known) this never seems to break the K9 spirit.

One can occasionally see the question asked on social media: "Do pets know they are in captivity?" The response generally covers subjects including whether they ever knew life in the wild and consideration of the nature of the captivity.

I can say with certainty Charlie knew she was in a benevolent captivity. It is hard to describe all of the ways in which one could reach such a conclusion around her, but it didn't take long. She certainly knew she and humans were not of the same species.

She knew that she was sometimes restrained from approaching other dogs, even though it was quite obvious that being in the company of others of her kind was generally her preference. She would stand on her hind legs and pull on the leash to try to get to them.

Separation was often kept because her response nose to nose with another K-9 was sometimes unpredictable. It might signal excited greeting and being ready to play. She could decide in an instant she didn't like what she was seeing, smelling or sensing and start to growl. She might hump the visitors's nose (generally not well received). This girl knew what she liked and what she was ready to reject.

Some dogs and dog breeds can be left without a leash and just follow their humans everywhere. She was not one of those. Charlie would run to what caught her eye, or pursue her distraction and go off on her own if an occasion arose.

Far from pitiful in her captivity, she clearly was loving

and affectionate with her people, but she always made a point to exercise her will to remind us that she had one.

For example, if one human companion called her, she might just look them right in their eyes and run to the other.

She refused to chase or fetch and would have nothing to do with a rolling ball. At the front window, she would bark for recognition at some dogs passing with their owners on the sidewalk, but not at others. She rarely barked in the same way at humans passing without pets.

This little Schnauzer knew her humans. She clearly preferred the company of women. Certain women she loved could drive up in front of the house and Charlie would be screaming with delight at the window. There were other friends who, despite their frequent visits, never got such a greeting.

Her interesting self-awareness of preference came to light with the "tucking in" ritual. This started when on a colder night we wrapped a soft little doggie blanket around her and kissed her goodnight. She curled up, put her little face on her front paws and instantly fake sleep.

It became a nightly ritual. Pat her spot on the bed, she would run to take her place and the tucking-in followed. So cute, right! So sweet!

As it turned out, as soon as she thought we were asleep, she would crawl out from under the little blanket and go to a favorite spot at the foot of the bed and sleep.

One night following this discovery, I simply tapped what I knew was her favorite place at the foot, with no tuck in. She looked over at the little blanket, gave me a knowing glance, happily curled up in her favorite spot and the game of playing along with the humans' "tuck-in thing" was over.

Sometimes our little dog could be quite overt about her

preferences. Generally, she paid little attention to the digital pads and phones at which we stared much of the time. On rare occasion, she would simply walk up, slap the phone or pad from one's hand, push it aside and crawl into a now empty lap. This might just be to cuddle there for thirty minutes looking out the window. Frequently, this displacement of the digital device was too sudden, too surprising, and too funny to disallow.

It all serves as a reminder that even the smallest creature can thrive more heartily with an occasional acknowledgement of their personhood. For Charlie, it might have been prompted by a gentle touch of a paw on one's leg. Just a simple recognition of her effort with a pat or a snuggle could send her wiggling or strutting away with her spirit lifted. It is a signal that recognizes, "I am here, and I matter."

The same is true of our children or our friends. Just to stop what one is doing and make a gesture to acknowledge, affirm and embrace another's personhood and identity with some sign of affection and recognition can go a long way toward lifting spirits. Animals (and people) deprived of recognition and affection can become adrift and depressed.

This is one thing dogs do for us as humans (sometimes, even when no one else does). They affirm our presence and our personhood. Whether it is by excitedly meeting us at the door, following us from room to room, reacting to our mood, sleeping under our desks while we work, or just a knowing look in our direction, it is life affirming. For some people it may be life saving. Just a little affirmation of presence and value is a big deal!

FIVE

Breaking
_____

**It was Charlie's first trip to the beach. She was
thrilled!**

Refusing to get her paws wet, Charlie excitedly but
strategically ran right at the surf's edge. It was her fully-
invested, thrilling run that exuded glee through every pore.
Her whole body wagged.

It was a busy public beach and she was on a leash, but

I kept up amid a lot of pulling and surging from her. We had a great time!

When we returned to the umbrellas where we were beaching with our companions for the day, a friend was frowning.

"I can't believe you let her drag you all over the place," she said. "You need a 'gentle leader' to break her to a leash and walking beside you."

Humans name things for our own purposes and feelings. A "Gentle Leader" is a contraption that goes around a dog's head and around its snout, and is designed to "control the dog's head so it can be pointed toward the owner when needed" (so says some of the promotion).

This little soul we called "Charlie" had been lifted as a baby from her doggie family of origin, had one litter of her babies taken from her, lost another litter in childbirth and almost died in the subsequent surgery.

Next, she had been taken from the human family that she loved, and now she somehow needed to be "broken" by me? I wouldn't think so! It was my opinion she was broken enough.

I launched into rather of a diatribe as to how I had no intention of snout binding at the beach this beautiful, intelligent, loving and self-aware creature in a way that would break her further to my will. I was determined to respect her dignity more than that.

I mentioned my own reluctance to even having her on the collar and leash she had grown up with, but felt like it was for her own protection.

My declarations were not well received by the party of the day.

Since that discussion I have given a lot of thought to this idea of "breaking" another individual. We break animals, we break children, we break work subordinates, we break our loved ones. We break little helpless populations in little helpless countries. We as humans are breakers.

Sometimes we religiously talk about "brokenness" as a good thing. We use the term "'breaking point." Many of us have memories of the various points as children when we were broken.

Some are more broken than others, and some spend their entire lives trying to repair the brokenness. Some violently lash out at the breakers and spend their lives in angry upheaval.

I thought about the idea that we have levels of pet breaking exemplified by this "Gentle Leader." It is a step beyond a collar and a leash. Next step, a choker chain, then a spiked choker chain, then a shocking collar. We humans are experts at breaking. The stronger the resistance, the more painful the breaking, until we create our idea of a gentle and compliant soul.

Look around at our society. How often is gentle too often synonymous with broken, and how costly is it that we sacrifice self-expression, glee, personality and full contribution in exchange for broke? We break men to Stoicism and women to cuteness. We break children through harrowing schedules of organized play.

We are recently in a whole world political movement to make sure we are all broken to a "gentle leader" of obedience, sameness and cowering conformity. We are also near a breaking point in human survival and experience.

At the beach, it was beyond the point of whether I would break my little furry K-9. She had already by the time we reached the beach been subdued by pet expectations. What we as her newer humans could do is to make a choice not to break her further.

It is a choice, by the way. It is a choice with animals

and it is a choice with children. How broken do we want them to be?

What I learned from Charlie is that where one draws the breaking line can make a huge difference in the mutual love, affection, respect and soul-to-soul interaction that can exist with proper boundaries and respect for dignity.

It is true with humans' relationship with their dogs. It is true with parents' relationship with their children. Exactly how much breaking do we want?

Establishing those boundaries is a dance, not a war. Some societies in our world have learned that. Unfortunately too many have not.

Some animals can never be broken and remain in the wild or in cages. The same is true of some people. Certainly, there were times when Charlie has had to yield her will to ours. It was done with expression and posturing that gave us a clear message that she knew this was happening. We knew it was out of love and respect, but she was clearly aware (and made us aware) of her every bending to our will.

If for example after a midnight pee excursion she was directed back to the bedroom instead of the kitchen for a snack, she would drop her ears and her head and grudgingly comply, but there was little guess that she had been coerced to do it. There was no mistaking that she had a clear expression of pouting attitude about it.

Perhaps there were things in Charlie's behavior that required special consideration and attention. Maybe there were things that could have been "broken" from her and made our lives easier. What a sad sacrifice that would have been!

Keeping those unbroken elements yielded the most loving, expressive, intelligent, devoted, creative, constantly fascinating and beautiful manifestations of personality and companionship one could find.

This brings the question of "how broken is broken enough?" We need to be asking that with our animals, we need to be asking that of ourselves, asking it about our influences, about our society and about our world. I wonder just how much more creative, dynamic and powerful human expression and contribution would be if we all got a better understanding of the impacts of brokenness.

Just how broken do we want our pets to be? How broken do we want our children to be? How broken do we want our companions or our society to be? Where does brokenness become ruin?

What is that line between simply civilized or broken and enslaved?

I have known one little dog whose droopy ears and side-eye glance could tell you instantly.

SIX

Boundaries

She has her boundaries

It was an hellacious uproar! Cutting through an early summer evening, Charlie's barks, growls, and wailing must have been heard for a mile away. When we spotted her, she was standing about two thirds of the way toward the back of our (near half-acre) lot. Very near the rather flimsy old four-foot chain link fence, she was screaming at something in the yard next door.

Her back feet were both churning. As she dusted like an angry bull, rocks and dirt were flying behind her.

Not ten feet on the other side of the fence was a very large, old, scruffy and very mean-looking coyote four times Charlie's size.

Charlie was now bouncing up and down as she dusted, let out-blood curdling growls and repeatedly charged at the fence. Although fully aware that a full-grown coyote can easily scale a four-foot chain link fence, Charlie's humans ran weaponless to her defense.

I lowered my voice and screamed obscenities at the intruder, but he didn't budge. Finally, when we started picking up large rocks and hurling them, the coyote (that we assumed by now was sick and crazy) slowly skulked into the underbrush.

What was abundantly clear was that our beloved little Charlie would not have given way. Even if the predator had scaled the fence, there was no doubt she would have defended her territory, even to the death if she had to.

We knew the coyote was probably sick and crazy

There was a motion-triggered light in that part of the yard. At nine that night we noticed the coyote was back. We assumed this time with some back-up buddies hiding in the brush. Within two weeks, an eight-foot privacy fence surrounded the entire property.

What had become unmistakable was that our little seventeen-pound dog was absolutely fearless in protecting her boundaries and would invest every ounce of her being and persona in that protection. There was not one trace of cowardice in her; not a hint of willingness to give an inch. It seemed not even to be an option.

Just as she protected and demanded respect for her own boundaries, Charlie recognized the boundaries of others.

It was later than we usually set out for her walk. Street-lights were already on, casting deep shadows in the evening. There was darkness around the corners and we were brightly highlighted on the walkway. Suddenly, just as we passed a big shrub, Charlie froze. There in the darkness, no more than six feet away, stood a huge buck.

His antlers were towering, and his chest loomed enormous beside us.

None of the three of us ever made a sound. The dog didn't bark. The buck didn't snort. I didn't throw up.

Slowly, Charlie and I turned and went back the way we came. Everyone's boundaries were quietly respected and we all went on to enjoy this beautiful evening. The buck slowly crossed the street behind us and we turned right at the next corner.

We walked the block and a half back to the house. As we started up the driveway, Charlie stopped silently again.

There was no barking, no posturing. There in the dark shadows was that same huge buck.

Then a strange thing happened. Charlie and the buck locked eyes and my heart stopped. Then they each raised their heads slightly, almost in acknowledgement, turned aside and slowly walked away from each other. "This," I thought, 'Is how boundaries are supposed to work."

Frequently, boundaries for us as humans are set or destroyed by the level of, and manner of brokenness we experienced as children. The same is true for animals. They growl, or they bark, or they run or cower at the sign of intrusion or threat often based on their past experiences.

Some people find their whole lives devoted to posturing and their own kind of barking to keep intrusion at bay. We build our psychological fences and dare anyone to cross them. Some of those with an excess level of harsh breaking in their lives, vow never to be broken further and live lives of guarded emotional isolation.

Others, seem to find some kind of comfort in the testing of others. They seem to want to reel in the potential for affection, then create an artificial opportunity for a breach, so they can lash out at the self-imagined new source of their brokenness. Thus, they are playing and replaying betrayal and abandonment in situations of their own making.

I know people who had their personal boundaries breached so definitively, harshly and intrusively when they were children that they have no idea what good healthy boundaries are supposed to look/feel like. It becomes a perpetuation of their own setting up of insult by violating the boundaries of others, often triggered to underscore their own expectation of intrusion.

Some explode into booming anger at the slightest perception of violated boundaries, thus triggering a violent reaction, a cumulative lashing out at every insult endured over a lifetime. This is often targeted at those who love them most. This short fuse can often cost jobs and destroy relationships.

Healthy boundaries are those based on a self-respecting and reasonable expectation of autonomy and protection. They are based on the reality of the moment and not the intrusions of the past. Some humans have no idea how to set them or how to respect them in others.

It's probably safe to suggest that at least some part of this boundary setting is instinctive in animals (at least if they haven't had it beaten out of them). The same, one would suppose, is true for people.

Our friend Jeff unknowingly created a full test for Charlie's boundaries. Once, when we knew we were going to be out much of the day, Jeff agreed to get Charlie and take her to his house to play with their two dogs. It all seemed to go without incident.

Jeff picked up Charlie and later returned her.

But now, the next time Jeff came for a visit, this Charlie who had always noisily and excitedly run to greet him and nuzzle her face against his beard, kept her distance. She seemed to want nothing to do with him. This went on for about a year, until suddenly one day she had clearly forgiven his trespasses. She was back to hugging and playing with Jeff just like before.

Everything returned to normal, except for one behavior. Generally when friends started to leave, Charlie would walk them to the door, even pulling back the curtain and looking out the front window to watch them get in the car.

Now with Jeff, whenever he started to leave, Charlie would go across the room and stand under the baby grand piano.

There she would stay, solidly seated and staring at the front door until Jeff had driven away. It was a subtle signal, but as clear as could be. There was no way she was going to get purloined again. She had her boundaries.

SEVEN

To Love A Dog

"Whoever declared that love at first sight doesn't exist has never witnessed the purity of a puppy or looked deep into a puppy's eyes. If they did, their lives would change considerably."[1]

Elizabeth Parker, *Paw Prints in the Sand*

Statistics show that 88.8% of pet owners view their pets as a "member of the family."[2] We can be pretty sure that is with a tendency toward attribution of human characteristics to those animals.

One important lesson I learned from Charlie is that the first and most vital step in loving a dog is to understand their dogmanity.

Archeological evidence suggests that dogs have been engaging in some kind of relationship with humans for at least 14,800 years.[3] All of those years, and we still don't appreciate fully who they are.

Dogs are not people. Despite our efforts to transfer all kinds of people characteristics, feelings and motivations to

them, they are products of a
different genetic makeup and a
whole other set of instinctive
drivers and physical and
sensory inputs to their brains.

Who knows how genera-
tions of being away from the
wild and being influenced by
humans may have changed the instincts, but a lot of the
nature from thousands of years is encoded in our dogs.
The dimension in which dogs live is very distinct from
our own.

Generally, no human can be perfectly happy to stay at
your side almost motionless, and watch a doorway to
instinctively guard you for two hours while you take an
afternoon nap. That is a pack animal with an inward sense
of responsibility and devotion to the pack. Dogs can have a
strong guardian impulse.

Feeding their social behavior, dogs take in a world that
creates a dimension for them that is in some ways much
more rich than ours. That dimension is a busy realm fed by
not only their sense of vision and of hearing, but a totally
different level of perception experience and a (still not
entirely understood) spatial and sensory sensitivity (some
provided by their vibrissae [whiskers]).

Given all of their capabilities, dogs have an innate
ability for emotional sensing and, for many, a high level of
emotional intelligence.

The whiskers are ultra-sensitive sensory organs and
are quite integrated into the total understanding a dog

gets from assessing its surroundings. It is thought that they provide navigation as well as spatial awareness. Although experts warn against cutting the whiskers as being painful and debilitating for a dog, it happens all the time to pets.

Then there is the magical nose! Dogs, not humans can take an olfactory tour of the neighborhood.

Humans can't even come close. Where humans may have some six million sensory receptor sites in our noses, it is said that a Beagle may have over three hundred million.[4]

In one spot, a dog can tell what has been there, what happened there, what was left there and a whole lot about the participants in all that went on, just from a sniff. From that previous visitor's level of sexual signaling to a sign of anxiety and more, the dog gathers information in ways we can't even imagine.

Better than a sommelier assessing a fine wine, dogs can evaluate molecules of days-old urine in ways we could never simulate.

We have all seen dogs at the airport who can sniff for the small little molecules of traces of explosives. Researchers are now enhancing training exercises so such dogs can better detect some substances that are combined in another form.[5]

Much like a million times enhancement of the wine expert, the dog has a routine of drawing in, holding, assessing, evaluating, and submitting the odor to a combination of internal mechanisms for judgement. A larger portion of the dog brain is devoted to processing and making sense of odors than that of humans' brains.

Dogs can hear frequencies we humans can't

Then there is the dog's hearing. While humans can hear sounds from 20 Hz to 20,000 Hz, dogs can pick up frequencies as high as 65,000 Hz. That means dogs may surprise us by reacting to sounds we don't even hear.

The Dog dimension is an intricate combination of computing and combining data from extremely data rich nasal and olfactory features, vibration and atmosphere sensitive whiskers as well as special sight, taste, and hearing.

Bottom line is, they do not experience the world in the

same way we as humans do. In short, they sacrifice a great deal of their reality to live in the confining dimensions of our humanized world.

We humans sometimes assign extraordinary special powers to our dogs. "They can read minds, are psychic specialists, are little psychiatrists," we humans might think.

Fact is, they actually can know things about us we may not even know about ourselves. They pick up on the most subtle of smells, and movements and changes to the environment our bodies and hormones create.[6]

Dogs have been trained to spot diseases and oncoming seizures. They can also spot scents created by changes in mood or circumstance.With all of their extraordinary special powers, dogs generally have no generational teaching on how to use them, and many do not have in their human home a companion who can share, understand and mutually enjoy such powers. In many homes, they are on their own. They are quite the misfits, but generally working hard to fit in.

We humans chop their whiskers, often pull their noses away before they finish processing precious odor data, douse them in noxious bug preventative mists, and bathe them with odiferous shampoos.

This makes it quite a miracle that they have adapted to interact so exquisitely with our expectations and companionship. Giving love that a dog appreciates includes recognition and accommodation of these special-dimensional and instinctive differences in them.

There are a lot of writings about how to take all this into consideration in loving our dogs. What we can add is that a little perceptiveness can allow one to read the signals as to what the dog likes best. For example, love your dog by letting him/her smell fully and richly, at least once in a while without interruption.

I learned from Charlie that, amid all of these differences in dimension and perception, we as human and dog can actually, genuinely love each other. That's where the miracle happens!

Extrapolating that to our human relationships, I have realized how differently human individuals perceive our own worlds.

Most of human conflict grows out of failure to recognize the reality of individuals, ages, generations, societies, genders, language, ethnic and experiential differences that cause us to live and understand the world in different ways, in often quite different dimensions. Every human lives in their own perceptive dimension, seeing the world as it is defined by their own experience.

Life well lived is a constant experience of learning. To learn outside of our own expectations and bias can open surprising new understanding and trigger beautiful and valuable human interaction. This leads to more opening of awareness and new vistas. Herein is the secret of becoming a mature, insightful and wise individual.

We can learn to mesh our various dimensions and realities, or we can too frequently bristle like a confused and angry dog that has based its entire set of perceptions on a bad ass sniff.

In our world today, there is entirely too much sniffing and bristling going on.

EIGHT

Allowing Love

Many of us believe we know how to shower love on a dog. For that matter, many of us believe we know how to shower love on our companions.

What is rare is the ability to allow oneself to be loved.

Some people discover this as they mature into relationships. Some never figure it out. How many times have we heard, "Oh there is no way she can love me as much as I love her." Or we have heard, "There is no way he can love me as much as I love him," or "sometimes I think I just fall too hard or love too much."

Some humans can literally smother another with what they believe to be their affection, but never in their lives have learned to allow themselves to be loved.

Sometimes they end up paired with someone who doesn't know how to give love (often with disastrous results). Imagine being a child with those two as parents.

The smothering folks often begin to turn the gestures of loving into tests. How receptive was the recipient? Did they tire and turn away? These testers sometimes set themselves up for rejection that they prompt and anticipate. This can be because they never fully know what the opposite of rejection is and don't understand what one should expect of another in a healthy relationship.

Dogs can be particularly perceptive in the presence of these affection tests and might just walk away.

How many people do you know who can just fold their arms in front of them, lean their head and body into the arms of another and allow a lover to calmly caress and hold them? This ability to be silent and still, and allow oneself to be loved is a gift many never find.

The aggressiveness and excitement of sex sometimes obscures this for humans' interactions with each other. Some people are somehow conditioned to experience sex or even a non-sexual love encounter as a more one-sided initiative.

All of us know people who are constantly posturing and performing, messaging, "love me, love me, love me." At the same time they are making it very clear that even if you wanted to genuinely love them, it would not be allowed.

Those people should never have a dog!

From Charlie, I was gifted with the revelation that animals can have a deep sense of quiet, admiring and contagious affection. This sweet spirit in her has been known to put our friends to sleep on the couch with her in five minutes.

There is an amazing adaptive emotional intelligence in our dogs. It is no surprise that research has shown children with a dog by their side react more positively in response tests when exposed to stress situations than do those with no dog.[1]

Many people with pets can be shocked to find what can happen if you sometimes just let the animal take charge of the loving.

(And by the way, for those of you with sick minds, this is not a leg humping reference.)

My pleasant surprises with Charlie have included when she silently pushes the cold and wet tip of her nose onto the back of my hand several times in repetition, then just leaves it there for fifteen seconds or so. It's is a sweet gesture that, well received, is given with grace and gentleness. It is one that has to be allowed.

If Charlie were to find a resting, palm-down hand, she might just put her face on it, press hard with her cheek and fall asleep.

The other expression is a gentle touch of the paw. It can signal a lot, but often can also be just a show of affection. She might reach over and just tenderly place a paw on one's leg, or wake in the morning and gently put two front paws on one's arm. Sometimes, there can be a very deliberate and soulful look in the eye, accompanied by the emission of three deep and beautiful Schnauzer grunts, as if to convey affection and assurance.

If one is quite still and very lucky, a dog may whisker you. This is when they delicately touch just their whiskers to you imparting a tingling, seemingly electrical impulse. It is a lovely feeling. And (if one believes in magic) a little impartation of special doggie emotional powers.

These gestures and dozens more are soft and beautiful expressions I would have never received if I always felt obligated to shower her with love and never allowed the quiet opportunity for Charlie to love me in her own way.

These creatures are famous for their doggie romps, slurppy licks, excited barks and tail wagging nuzzling expressions of excited affection. To discover the more profound, spiritual experience with a dog, means opening the space and allowing oneself to be loved with that special silent mode of loving they reserve for those who let them in.

I believe the same is true of people. Unfortunately, some never discover this truth.

NINE

Exuberance!

Men shouldn't giggle and women can't guffaw.

We humans are pitifully socially constrained in the level to which we can show exuberance. The imposition of constraint or acceptance of joyful abandon can vary by geographic area and ethnic expectations. It can also vary by how much an individual is broken in ways discussed in an earlier chapter.

Unless humans make them "highly-trained" or overly break them, dogs have a wonderful ability to pull out all the emotional stops and explode into an unconstrained display of exuberance that is an inspiring, joyful and contagious sight to behold. It's one reason humans love them so.

We are obsessed with the pups. A survey by *Kelton Global, a* leading global insights research firm conducted for *BarkBox and Company* revealed that on average, those with a dog post a picture or talk about their dog on social media six times per week.

One in ten have created a social media account just for their dog.

The study also found that twenty percent of the pictures people take on their phones are of their dog and forty-two percent have made a photo of their dog the home screen photo on their phone or computer.[1]

In many cases, these photos are of dogs in states of exuberance. We as humans love it when our dogs jump or spin or pant or squeal with excitement when they see us or in response to various stimuli. Maybe it's because they show joy in ways we are constrained from displaying in our own delight.

It is also true that we can baby talk, and coo and high-pitched exclaim to them things in ways we couldn't otherwise, because somehow talking to a dog gives us permission to become childlike.

Happily, our Charlie has never been overly constrained from her exuberance.

When someone she liked pulled into the driveway, she might be seen standing in the window bouncing up and down squealing with delight. When they walked in, her whole body would wiggle and gyrate with excitement at seeing them.

After a bath, she traditionally broke into an unbridled and full-throttle mad run. Ears blowing back and flopping and tongue extended, quietly, but excitedly she circled the yard with uncanny speed, brimming with happiness. (Sadly, this had to be dialed back some with her heart disease, but not much.)

On playdates with her puppy friends, there was an endless display of running and thrilled delight.

When it was obvious her meal bowl was being prepared, Charlie dusted with her back feet and bounded with excitement.

Guess some people prefer quiet, soft-mannered, more polite dogs. What a waste! Catching contagious joy from a dog is a treasure and a treat.

We as humans might take some lessons from them.

Theorists disagree on just how much our cultural and ethnic influences impact the expression of human emotions. Some even argue that different segments of our species actually feel and experience emotion differently.[2]

One thing learned from Charlie is that we could probably all benefit from more joy and by granting ourselves greater permission to express our own glee. How sad that some people blush when they laugh out loud!

Unfortunately, we are becoming more and more of a society that discourages any humor in the course of doing business and views lightheartedness as not taking the job seriously, or as just wasting time.

Maybe a need for perceived permission to break out of our emotional confines is why people are now going in record numbers to South America to unbridle their emotions by doing Ayahuasca and other hallucinogenic substances.

Maybe our usual pent-up approach to emotion is why so many people smoke marijuana or eat gummies to trigger what is readily recognizable as "the giggles."

It is all so much more acceptable than just bursting into laughter, *au naturel* and unconstrained. "Oh I am so stoned," is such a wonderful and freeing explanation of a sudden release of joyfulness.

Perhaps, if a natural outburst of exuberance and giggles were more socially acceptable, we wouldn't need quite as much drug use in our society to permit us to occasionally "let loose."

Imagine a world where we were allowed, even encouraged, to break into excited bouncing, laughing and joy when one of our favorite people drove into the driveway to visit.

There actually is a science that is the study of our chuckles. Gelotology is dubbed the scientific study of laughter. Our laughing is quantifiably good for our health. It acts psychologically on many parts of our body. Impacting us physically and hormonally, laughter has been shown to bring positive results to human health and psyche. It can even increase pain tolerance.[3] It truly is good for the soul!

A number of studies have confirmed that mirth can maintain and even restore our health. Why then do we approach stress, illness and problems with such solemnity? This is probably because our society is such that laughing through any of this would get us categorized as "whack jobs" and might get us put away.

I learned much from watching Charlie cut through illness, pain and loss with her brave episodes of exuberance. It has been a powerful lesson of how expressions of joy at life's littlest blessings can be so healing and redemptive.

When my mother died, members of her family of origin stayed later one night than everyone else. These were people who had grown up on a farm, out in the middle of nowhere in Oklahoma during the Depression. They were about to show my sister and I something about dealing with adversity.

Mom's sisters and brothers shared stories of growing up. They relived all of the fun and funny moments. For several hours, the room was filled with beautiful and unbridled laughter. Those were the most healing moments of the entire experience, and moments of which my mother would have been extremely proud.

It could be quite amazing how a little more human buoyancy could change our world.

TEN

Expiration Date

We all have an expiration date.

Once, Charlie had one officially assigned to her.

It started with an apparent urinary tract infection (UTI). A lot of medical testing resulted in a trip to a veterinary oncologist, a cancer diagnosis and a pronouncement that it was inoperable.

Charlie had urinary tract cancer. "With 'intensive treatment,' she can live maybe three to six months," said the oncologist. It was clearly a verdict that Charlie soundly rejected outright.

She could't tolerate the "intense treatment." Over a couple of weeks of vomiting and diarrhea, she was wasting away and ended up taking just a dietary supplement treatment instead.

With the UTI cleared and the intense treatment discarded, Charlie returned to a pretty much normal routine, except that our relationship with her became a lot more tender and precious. The knowledge that we may lose her helped emphasize how loved and how valuable to us she was.

No one can be sure what she knew, but Charlie returned the tenderness and seemed to tune in to the reality of our knowing she had terminal cancer.

A friend who taught nursing once said that one of the greatest healing forces humankind has is being "surrounded with a white light." "Nurses learn this in the real world," she told us. "They see a difference in their patients when self-healing attitudes change as those patients learn to find their white light." She also said we can extend the virtues to surround others with our own "white light."

Although there are well-known healing qualities to actual lighting. This internal version is not literal in the strictest sense of the word, but it can be very real.

This nursing professor taught her classes how to close one's eyes and draw from the depths of one's soul to call forth a great white light that she said resides in us all. "With some practice, one can see, feel and sense the power of the light," she would say.

Actually, the practice has a basis in neuroscience. Accessing positive imagery can open pathways in the brain that have curative physical impacts in the body. There is not a much more positive summoning of energy than one intensely imaging a great internal white light.

Can one hold another and share that energy? We decided with Charlie it was worth a try. Whether or not it worked, it did bring quiet and soulful moments between us that always seemed to recharge her. She would go bounding from the embrace with a seeming sense of renewal and joy.

The exercises also brought a bit of healing to our sadness over her condition.

Charlie's six-month expiration date flew past.

At about ten months, she had just finished a bath and had launched into her traditional unbridled, full-throttle post-bath run when suddenly she just fell over on the back deck. Legs stiffened, eyes rolled back, it seemed sure she was gone.

In a couple of minutes, this little miracle stood, shook herself and walked on into the yard. As it turned out, this had been a case of syncope.

Another vet visit and another series of tests revealed a leaky heart valve with a resultant enlarged heart and heart failure. Was she in pain? Seemingly, no. Could she be cured? No. She could be treated with medication.

Diuretics could pull fluid off the lungs and a certain cardiac stimulant could encourage better heart efficiency.

The medication seemed to return Charlie to a pretty much normal life. It allowed us a measure of denial, and life went on. She had a great appetite, she announced when it was time for her walk. She nuzzled and expressed joy. Whatever the inconvenience of disease, she pressed through it seemingly without complaint.

Through it all, most impressive was the quiet gentleness and resolute knowingness she exuded. Her entire set of sunset moments in her life seemed to be just permeated with loving and trust.

The catch (if there was one) was that this little patient had to pee every three or four hours or so, or the fluid would build in her lungs and around her heart and she would die. Given that we were in an area surrounded by wild animals and Charlie was mostly deaf and poor-sighted, this middle-of-the-night peeing needed some human companionship.

It meant working in shifts to make sure she could go outside during the night. How reasonable is it for humans to be this devoted to a dog to do this for months? My friend, you would have to know the dog.

More than a year past the pronouncement of the timing of her demise and with two terminal illnesses, Charlie was still happily living a rather normal life with a little help from friends. Although occasionally upset by little health flareups, she was pretty much oblivious to her overall condition. She was able to find plenty of moments of sheer delight and seek comfort in her daily routine.

For all of this to come together for Charlie, demanded a high level of devotion and investment from her people. It was devotion we were lovingly willing to give.

Is that strange in a human world with so many

conflicting values and prejudices? Maybe. Does it all make sense? Probably not. Is it worth it? Could a little Schnauzer be worth it? Absolutely!

ELEVEN

Animalistic!

It had been a particularly difficult week. I had worked long and tedious hours with a client that was being unreasonable.

Charlie had developed some adaptation of her diuretic dosage that at times, if we let her, she could just sleep through the hours from midnight to six in the morning.

At first we considered this a blessing, but then realized it only meant that her heart failure would continue to generate fluid that would fill her lungs. Now she ended up gasping for air having another incidence of syncope, and we had made another trip to the vet.

Having now learned this the hard way, we had to wake her every three hours or so and make sure she got up to go outside and pee. It was either this, or watch her drown in her own fluids. It was harsh, but very much for her own good. She was not always amenable to the waking.

This particular night, Charlie didn't really want to wake up. She was resistant and slow. I finally got her awake and fumbled to put on my shoes. Reluctantly, she followed me to the back door. It was freezing cold, windy and icy outside. The earlier trips out that night had been harrowing.

Just as I started to open the door, Charlie looked me right in the eye, stooped and peed on the carpet.

She looked me right in the eye and stooped to pee

In my three in the morning stupor, I interpreted it as saying, "You go out. I'm not going out in that cold mess after you woke me from a sound sleep."

Suddenly, I was furious. We went out anyway. As we walked the yard, I thought of all of the effort we were going through to keep her as healthy as possible.

"You little bitch! You don't appreciate it," I thought. Fact is, as long as we were steady with her medication and accumulated fluid emptying, she seemed to be staying pretty comfortable. Then, for the first time, I found myself thinking that it could all be brought to a halt. "Maybe, she will just die, or maybe we should end it."

Tired, cold and angry, I was looking at this sweet-spirited creature who had given nothing but love and devotion and a constant source of joy to us and thinking to end her life while she was perfectly capable of enjoying it with just a little medicine and help from her friends.

Then, in that bitter winter wind, I remembered how angry I had become at the vet when she had looked at me and kind of scolded, "you know people generally 'put a dog down' more for their own convenience, rather than to help the dog." I thought at the time she had really insulted me.

With my thoughts still swirling and while crunching through dangerous footing on ice I was suddenly remorseful. I hoped Charlie couldn't read my mind. Then I remembered my own ideas that human thought, released into the universe, has some power to influence reality. At this moment I hoped it wasn't true.

We walked inside. I took off my coat and my shoes to look up and see Charlie sweetly and politely looking over her shoulder with those big beautiful eyes to wait for me in the hallway on the way back to bed. I started to quietly sob. I held her for a few seconds and did my best to make up for my mean thinking by hugging her tightly. I cried.

In this moment of my own new awareness I realized what I might be willing to sacrifice for my own convenience or self protection. I carried part of the burden of decision making for another lovely creature's life.

For some time now, Charlie had gradually been enlightening me as to how we as humans misjudge animals. We have an entire and elaborate perception of what we think of as "animalistic."

Humans are highly species bigoted. This little dog had been teaching me that this bigotry plays out in our treatment of animals much like it plays out with people's treatment of each other.

We as humans tend to assign traits, characterizations and stereotypes across the board to entire genres, species, even divisions of human race and culture. We generalize and categorize and define what separates us from animals and even from other "kinds" of humans.

We tend to believe that, unlike the animals, we are soulful, and empathetic, knowing, sophisticated and even sacrificial in our devotion to each other and our world. We tend to think we, above all others, have a corner on intelligence, love and affection. We don't. Thinking so only serves to give us a sense of incredible license to be enormously cruel.

Here in one powerful moment on a freezing February night I had opened a door to reveal myself as a creature who was willing to prematurely kill someone he dearly loved just for convenience. I had come to consider Charlie a bit of a little ambassador and envoy that was progressively giving me more insight into her animal community. Tonight was a big lesson.

We went to bed and Charlie went back to sleep. I didn't.

Wide awake now, my mind wandered through the hypocrisy of humanity. I was heartbroken over this one little loving creature, while at the same time, living in a home with a freezer full of meat.

My thoughts went back to the "killer" Charlie protecting her boundaries by once shaking a squirrel to death. I wondered where barbarism resided and where loving civility prevailed. What was her instinctive guiding light for propriety?

How much of us as humans is savage animal, and how much variability is there in that from person to person?

We love our "pets." We acknowledge their powerful love and devotion for us. Some hunters take their beloved dogs with them to retrieve the little helpless, cooing doves they just shot out of the air with a sixteen-gauge shotgun.

(Later, I learned that various sources confirm that just Americans spend almost 150-billion dollars a year on pets.)

We love on them. We talk about how smart and cute and cunning they are. We confide in them and are comforted by them. Some get emotional support from them.

We compartmentalize species according to our own biases. People can become incensed that in Asia some may eat dogs. We can be intrigued by the fact that an octopus is so intelligent, sentient, thoughtful and creative. We can think, "wow they are smart enough to open a jar lid," then we eat one as sushi. It is widely reported that about eighty-percent of the world's species have not yet even been discovered. How fortunate for them. It means people aren't eating them.

In my wide-awake night, my mind went back to when I was five-or-six-years-old and we had chickens. Occasionally, my sister and I would be in the backyard and our mother would come marching out the back door and to the chicken pen.

She would grab a chicken barehanded and wring its neck. Then she would pluck it, clean it and take it back into the house to prepare for dinner.

Mom always warned, "Don't name the chickens!" We did anyway. This meant that if Henrietta were coming for dinner, she was there FOR dinner. (or the same for Clara Cluck, or, my favorite, Cockadoodle Sue).

Such a scene in front of children might horrify people today. I think, however, that in the whole process my sister and I learned something about the sacrifice animals make to sustain humans.

We humans can woo and coo our way through

hundreds of cute animal pictures on social media. We show adorable videos of everything from pets to farm animals and wild creatures engaged in every comedic, endearing and entertaining antic imaginable.

We delight in anything that suggest human-like reactions or qualities in animals.

We love cute little animal pictures on social media

Fact is, that we as a species kill off a staggering amount of life in our world. We kill and eat (or waste) literally trillions (with a "t") of sentient beings annually.

Humans slaughter for food 900,000 cows per day; 140,000 chickens every minute.[1]

Humans kill and eat one billion rabbits a year.[2]

At the same time, the consumers of all of this spend an estimated 31 billion dollars a year in veterinary bills for their pets.[3] We have powerful species-specific bias when it comes to other living creatures.

We have a most profound, dramatic and confusing human perception of what, which and how much we "value life." We are worse than animals, because we kill for sport, for greed and for prestige. We also waste tons of what we supposedly kill for food. Some declare themselves "pro-life" while supporting detached participation in murderous cruelty.

The output of our carnage is parceled out in pretty paper, colorfully printed wrappings, or brightly lit chilled cabinets in markets. The raw truth is that humans are kept alive by a daily ritual of animal sacrifice. We deny it, we obscure it and sweep it under the carpet of our awareness, but sacrifice sustains us.

...and this little piggy stayed home!

Coming to an understanding of all of this, one would think I would become a vegan, but I too have so much residual beast in me I always succumb to a craving for flesh. I am a member of the most voracious, indiscriminate and wasteful murderous predator class on Earth. Probably, my sin is that I know it. We as humans will dine at every layer of the food chain. We have even been known to eat each other.

In all of this, we are carefully protected from the underlying truth that we are the most dangerous of animals who may strangely be willing to mount a three-thousand-dollar vet bill to keep a little creature we cherish alive and happy.

Indigenous people used to have ceremonies before meals to express gratitude to their fallen game. Soldiers came along and piled dead buffalo carcasses into mountains for the power of depriving the native landowners of their livelihood. In some ways (and at some times) we become worse than the beasts we belittle.

We have all seen the ads on television where unimaginable cruelties are shown with starving dogs on chains, or puppies abused with all manner of cruelty by humans. Unfortunately, animal abuse is a serious problem that reflects a tragic flaw and dark side in human character and upbringing.

The Humane World for Animals organization reports that animal abusers may frequently also be people abusers. Studies found that seventy-one percent of domestic violence victims reported that their abuser also targeted pets.

In one study of families under investigation for suspected child abuse, researchers found that pet abuse had occurred in eighty-eight percent of the families under supervision for physical abuse of their children.[4] Innocent dogs suffer at the hands of sadistic people who also have just as little respect for their children.

In fits of whimsy, we as humans sometimes talk about encounters with space aliens and fantasize how they might be different and how we might form an alliance with them. We (or they) had better hope they look exactly like us. We are surrounded on all sides by creatures of difference who are sometimes intelligent and fabulous, and (almost without exception) we have killed and eaten them.

In ways, this little dog I know somehow appears so much more civilized in the scheme of things.

With my tiny animal envoy Charlie sometimes curled up in the crook of my arm asleep at night, I continue to learn.

I have sometimes listened to her endearing sleeping sounds and thought of how the raccoons and squirrels, and even wolves lovingly snuggle close and purr as they sleep in their dens and pens.

Humans do not have an exclusive right to love and affection. What we do have, is a convenient denial of our savagery and some pretty packaging of our astounding bloody impacts.

Even with our barbaric track record as humans, we have pets.

If they ever only knew with whom (or what) they were dwelling, how could they ever relax by our side at night while we watch TV?

TWELVE

Civilized!

"Mankind invented the atomic bomb, but no mouse would ever construct a mousetrap."

Albert Einstein

We humans are so proud of how "superior" we are.

I have sometimes looked at Charlie and wondered which is the better species. Is it hers, that has lived for thousands of years in dignity and stability? Or, is it mine, that captured other humans, stacked them in their own sweat and urine and feces and shipped them thousands of miles so we could ultimately claim that we (who had committed that atrocity) "civilized" them?

Who exactly is the civilized among us? I wonder, Charlie, is it the ones who have devised means to instantly immolate our world, or to slowly condemn it to sure environmental death? Or is it the ones who live for centuries in balance and dignity with all around them?

But, let's think redemptively. Let's think of how humankind has perpetuated civilization in our world.

We have created some of the most sophisticated architectural wonders, we have brought innovations in medicine and engineering, biology, sociology and agriculture that can benefit all of life on Earth. The difference between us and the not-so-civilized is that we know how to come together to pool our resources to advance civilization and contribute to future generations.

**Humans have built architectural wonders
around the world**

For examples we can look to the United States. We can first examine a claim it is a country that knows how to support others not so fortunate in humanity by pooling its resources and helping fight starvation brought by famine and war by shipping tons of grain to the less fortunate. At the same time, this supports the nation's farmers by underpinning the grain markets. It can assure domestic food supply by keeping all the farmers in business.

But, wait! That's gone! The current US regime cut funding for that. It is estimated that by 2031 some fourteen million people will die as a result of cuts in U.S. Agency for *International Development (USAID)* funding cuts. It was just more civilization than a new U.S. regime felt necessary.

At any rate, another shining example of civilized is that the country put national resources together to fund an ability to monitor any outbreak of deadly disease anywhere in the world and send in a team of the finest clinical and science disease experts to nip it in the bud and help locals squelch the spread of the illness. This helps make sure these outbreaks don't become a pandemic and kill people around the world.

But, wait! They have cut funding for that.

Never mind, The U.S. also collectively as a society formed a policy to support farmers by buying their products and providing free breakfast at school for poorly supported children so their learning is fueled for the day and they can make society better. This has clearly been shown to have multiplied financial and sociological returns in underpinning future generations.

Oh, gosh! That went away in funding cuts.

It's okay! The future of civilization is still being served!

The U.S. as a society pooled its resources and made sure there was funding such that in universities all across the country the finest clinicians, scientists, engineers, biologists, sociologists and experts of all kinds were always engaging in cutting-edge research to move society forward. This would assure the constant advancement of what it means to be civilized. It has been lauded and respected worldwide.

Well hell! They defunded that too!

It's okay, the U.S. society sustained a department to make sure that there was consistent public education across the country for everyone. Regardless of how many challenges a child carried, schools were equipped to help that child be all they could be in life. Oh my God! They went in to close that down too?

The good news is that the country maintained a

department of experts who are devoted to making sure air and water are always safe and healthy for all of the Earth's creatures.

No! Instead of refining and focusing and supporting that mission, The latest U.S. regime cut the funding for much of that, erased any acknowledgement of global warming and pretty much paralyzed the effort.

But at least, always seeing itself as a leader of freedom, the U.S. stands for respecting boundaries. If one nation brutally and outlandishly attacks their neighbor, America might be the first to come to the victim nation's aid to protect the boundaries and rules of humane treatment. Whoops! Don't count on it. Allies are recently abandoned.[1]

The claim has been that the programs we mention here were defunded to save money for taxpayers, a boast that was made by a ruling political party that subsequently sought to add over four trillion dollars to the US national debt. It was claimed the programs were "woke."

Maybe the programs were simply civilized; the kind of thing civilized societies do to perpetuate civilization.

In an effort to conduct a culture warfare blitzkrieg, the latest US government (and some and a handful of other governments around the world) have taken a machete to funding for the arts, advanced learning, and Earth protection. A large contingent of modern society has decided to focus on only here and now, and abandon many potential contributions to future advancement of civilization.

Governments in many parts of the world are responding to a "me" and "now" focus of current generations by this abandoning funding of humanitarianism, creativity and the arts.

Maybe it is an undercurrent of belief that global warming precludes a distant future, but for whatever reason investment in civilized intellect and beauty that endures into future centuries has lost traction in society. A humanity that operates on a belief there is no future is one that may be destined to prove itself right.

Instead of those who sacrifice for freedom and human progress, the new heroes seem to have become the richest and most boastful and selfish among us.

Sadly, we have devolved lately toward being a wild pack, trying to brutally expand our territory. We have signed orders to banish the expansion of civilized evolution and moved to piss out new boundaries. We have piss-marked our territory of power with greed and brutality; with insane propaganda and the most debased of rhetoric.

Piss marking new territory

Some have caged and warehoused humans stacked in cells several stories high while standing in front of them with a thumbs-up sign and a big grin for a photo op.

The new value system seems to equate a person's level of human sophistication and value with only the measurement of being wealthy, arrogant and in power.

Is all of this something new? No, it is a cyclical manifestation of humanity's knee-jerk response when developments in the world start to break down our traditional understanding of reality.

The era of *The Dark Ages* was just such a response to society finding itself on the brink of a different social world order. When the power structure senses a shift in perspective, it stiffens and postures toward more base and selfish human tendencies.

It all goes to show us just how fragile our civilized society can become.

As a very young man, this writer was dispatched as a reporter on Christmas Day to cover an earthquake in Managua, Nicaragua. It was a hot day and soldiers were dragging bodies into the street and setting fire to them to prevent disease.

What was most impressive was how people were coming together to share resources and camping spaces. They were loving and generous, bound as humans by the suffering that had befallen them.

After nightfall, however, the streets rang with gunfire and screams, as a more evil element preyed on the helpless by looting and marauding, and some were shot by the police.

Sometimes civilization is a thin veneer. It can be breached by horrid natural catastrophe.

Sadly, it can also be breached by too much wealth, privilege, greed, dogma and arrogance. It can be breached by people who fear change, even if it is change for the better.

Like the feckless grasshopper in the well-known *"Ant and the Grasshopper"* parable, the current wave of self-indulgent leadership has become obsessed with satisfying a voracious appetite of the few and the moment, with little thought for longer-range benefits for the many. It is a selfish waste and devouring of what has been left for us by antiquity with no obligation to give back.

It is the sacrifice of this veneer of civilization that allows humans to become a very distinctly destructive and offensive kind of animal.

We as the human animal have the instincts to be better than this. Unfortunately, there have been times in history when leaders who came to power capitalized on humans' most basic greedy, lustful and insane tendencies. Only self-sacrifice, determination and devotion to the thread of civilized awareness can counter such a moment.

THIRTEEN

Take It All In

"The purpose of life, after all, is to live it, to taste experience to the utmost, to reach out eagerly and without fear for newer and richer experience."

Eleanor Roosevelt

It was a breezy spring day with thunderstorms brewing to the east. Newly sprouted leaves and flowers were lovely and fragrant.

As I stood on an upper deck watching her, Charlie walked to the highest part of the yard where there was a flower bed that was raised about three feet. She stood with her front feet together, raised her head skyward and looked up for a long time at the trees and the sky, the breeze stirring her whiskers and ears.

She was so clearly just absorbing it all, savoring the experience and fully alive in that spring moment. She stood for a long time so apparently immersed in the experience.

I watched thinking, "You go girl! It's such a miracle you are still alive and have your senses for this moment. Take it all in and savor it all."

That night during our usual TV watching time, Charlie had what was later presumed to be a mini-stroke and lost most of the vision in her left eye. One has to wonder if the scene earlier that day was a result of her sensing something was about to happen to her, or whether she just had drawn from her experience and circumstances over the past several months a compulsion to take life in in the fullest and most sensitive ways possible.

I will always have locked in my mind that image of Charlie standing in that breeze and absorbing the day with all her senses and be reminded in those moments where I should do that for myself.

We are all just fragile little bags of blood living in a sometimes harsh and prickly world. Every sensitivity is vulnerable and every moment with our fullest faculties is a gift. Yet we are all so busy.

We are too busy sometimes for meaningful friendships, too busy to take in the beauty of Spring, to have our senses bathed in any of the moments that wash over us, then disappear forever every day.

We would rather text than to hear the nuances in the

friendly voices of those we love. Unfortunately, too quickly we are becoming the technology that we use, and that removes us from the beautiful senses of our humanity.

The aura of human eye contact, the world of meaning in a subtle change of voice, the raised eyebrow, the cocked head, the gentle sigh; we are too busy for such full embrace of the human experience. "Get to the point and let me move on," often doesn't actually arrive at the real point being signaled at all.

Just as we jerk the leash when our walking dogs are stopping to take in a hugely-informative and message-ridden whiff, we nudge our children, "What tha hell are you looking at? C'mon we'll be late to soccer!" We do the same to ourselves, always too preoccupied or busy to let our senses fill and take in a moment. Everything is sooo important all the time!

Take It All In !

To climb to the highest spot. To stop, to look up, to feel the breeze and take it all in is a luxury we seldom allow ourselves or even others we love. We assume there will always be time for that later. Will there?

FOURTEEN

Life Forms

"Divinity reveals herself in all things. Everything has Divinity latent within itself. For she enfolds and imparts herself even unto the smallest beings, and from the smallest beings, according to their capacity.

Without her presence nothing would have being, because she is the essence of the existence of the first unto the last being."[1]

Giordano Bruno

The person who wrote the quote above lived in the 1500s.

He was a priest, a philosopher, a theologian and a highly respected academician.

Bruno (in the 1500s, mind you) suggested that each star was a sun and had planets circulating around it like our own sun. The idea that the Earth was not the center of the universe was considered heretical. Ultimately, Bruno's tongue was bound with a steel clamp and he was burned at the stake by the leaders of the Roman Catholic Church.

Since that time, of course, we have decided that Bruno was right about the stars. But, as far as The Church was concerned that was not his only "heresy." The quote shown here (attributed to the goddess Isis in this case, but appearing in other writings directly attributable to Bruno) that all things have divinity within them, was considered pantheistic and heresy. Of course, everyone knew that God was an old white man watching from heaven like an adult Elf on the Shelf[TM].[2]

While society and science are now sure about the stars, there is probably plenty of religious and secular challenge still about Bruno's suggestion of divinity of all things.

The pattern of living of humanity certainly doesn't lend itself to a recognition of divinity or God-ness in all creatures, Many might still consider Giordano a heretic for those views.

Evidence suggests he was probably right. Maybe in our troubled modern times when the Earth hangs in the balance, the holiness around us is trying to tell us something.

Think of this: There was once a gorilla named Koko who learned more than a thousand human words in sign language and communicated her emotions to humans. That is a generally well-known and publicized story.

What isn't so generally known is that her human

mentors were bombarded with criticism and attacked at every turn by an academic community anxious to deny that real communication was taking place. "Koko was mimicking and responding to rewards and feedback," the criticism said. Couldn't the same be said of human children learning a language?

Fact is, Koko could recognize herself in a mirror and sign her name in response. More importantly, she could tell humans how she felt. She expressed opinions and feelings.

Some prickly members of the scientific community became all aflutter challenging whether animals could convey such things. Clearly, those were people who never shared a household with a dog.

Koko expressed feelings and emotions in sign language

Despite all the criticism, Koko's experience seemed to introduce a new age in human and animal relations.

Now, a myriad of types and configurations of animal "communication button" kits are being sold online. Promoting "fluent" cats and dogs, the electronic buttons can be pushed individually by an animal to trigger specific audible human spoken words. The kits provide instructions on how to train one's pet to use them arrayed out in front of them to communicate in actual human language. There are even videos demonstrating this happening.

Dogs are given a set of buttons that can each play a human word

Dogs may learn and understand words differently than humans, but research has shown that smart dogs can learn and retain understanding of many human words. One study found that particularly linguistically brilliant dogs can learn ten or twelve new words a week.[3]

Are we witnessing a new age in recognition, or opening of communication and understanding between humans and animals? Or, are we simply newly living in a world where the presence of millions of online videos of animal and human interaction is underscoring what has always been there?

Lately, scientists are discovering that animals experience grief, mourning and existential dread as they have awareness of their own mortality.

In a world of barbarism, murder and aggression, has a chasm existed between animal and human relationships that various species may now be trying to span and heal?

Widespread internet video sharing is opening a whole new world. Wild sea otters tossing a ball to a little girl, huge whales clearly putting on a show for a boatload of tourists, sea mammals asking divers for help to untangle creatures from fishing nets may all be part of a start in weaving a story of a new age of interaction.

Grateful animals coming back or hanging around to thank their human rescuers convey purpose and emotion we have long believed to be only possessed by humans.

Thousands of videos seem to show animals trying to speak human words or parrots cussing a blue streak in a very purposeful and responsive way. A donkey laughs its ass off when a dog is shocked by an electric fence in a viral video that seems to clearly reflect an animal's sense of comedy.

An entire video documentary, *My Octopus Teacher*, is devoted to recounting a friendship between a man and an octopus in the wild. Appointments are kept, gifts are exchanged, thoughts are shared as this documentary follows the growing friendship[4]

Despite doubters, we are starting to get a view of species breaking through with efforts to make sense of each other.

As smart as we humans are, maybe we are dulled to sensitivities that many of our other fellow creatures on Earth share with each other. Maybe as the bloody predators we are, most of us have simply never been listening.

How ironic would it be if this age of breakthrough in interspecies understanding is taking place at a time when humans are rapidly destroying it all?

It is estimated that we are losing between 18,000 and 55,000 species to extinction each year in our world.[5]

Of the ones who are sentient, intelligent and have cognition, we will never know what they saw, we will never know what they thought funny and we will never know what they could teach us.

Sadly, we will never know what they found funny. Unfortunately, in our arrogance, we assume they could teach us nothing, and they won't be missed.

As brilliant as we humans believe we are, we are being stupid, stupid, stupid, stupid. We are stuck in a pervasive dominance mentality. We are motivated by an insatiable lust to satisfy a need for security by creating a realm that is woven of a perception of control by possession.

Consider that we now have weapons that can travel at ultrasonic speed to deliver a decisive blow thousands of miles away in an almost immediate fashion, yet we are still clinging to old-world ideas of needing to seize geographic stronghold points to export power in the world. Why are we bent on geographic staging for warfare when geographic bastions only fulfill an ancient perception of military advantage?

Why are humans willing to soil our own bedding of this Earth to build competitive advantages based on our imagination of political, social and economic borders?

We are on the cusp of a world where cerebrally implanted chips could open a whole new vista of human and even interspecies understanding. Yet, it is threatened with being unraveled by ancient rivalries, religions and archaic mentality.

Then there are dogs. They are probably the closest thing to human/animal hybrid we can find. After over 14,000 years living with us, they have learned to reflect our emotions, understand our language, mostly avoid being eaten and live in harmony with us like no other creatures can. They have shared devotion, love, humor and exuberance with us in intimate cohabitation for centuries. In some ways, they are more conscious than we.

Through centuries of deciding we are somehow becoming more and more civilized, we humans have only been developing ways to more efficiently, powerfully and effectively spread our barbarism.

Despite all of this, some people on social media are living in an entirely different realm where understanding, human contact, relationships, humor, enlightenment, love and appreciation are being spread across the artificial boundaries of geopolitical discourse. They are crossing societal boundaries to love, to laugh, to entertain, educate and unite in ways humanity has never experienced.

All of this, of course, cannot be allowed. In an effort to retain the old warrior social norms, earlier generation power mongers are doing everything they can to shutdown digital media or control it decisively.

They are digitally spreading dogma of ancient religions and social notions, many of which teach that specifically men are charged with dominating the Earth and all its creatures. They reinforce no longer needed gender, social and geographic dominance perceptions and sour the enormous potential we have right now for powerful evolution of our species.

It is strangely akin to dark ages goons trying to squelch with fear and clinched fists the dawn of any reformation. Sadly, in this case, the consequence may be the loss of all of creation's ability to thrive or survive.

To an extent, in the twenty-first century, we are no longer asking whether one believes in global warming. Climate change is a matter of fact. The only question now to be asked is whether we are beyond a tipping point of no return. The time to sit up and take notice to take preemptive action may be past.

Perhaps, we still have time to pay greater attention to the meaning, reality and precious nature of what we have and may be losing. We need to, as was said in the preceding chapter, "Take it all in."

As humans, our claim to power and dominance has always been an idea that in all the world we are the superior intellect. This, of course, has always been measured by our own intellectual standards and capabilities, totally discounting those of all other life on the planet.

Now, by our own making, we have supplanted our self-perceived intellectual dominance. Artificial Intelligence (AI) vastly exceeds humans' capabilities to obtain and retain knowledge. As AI gathers, sorts and digests all intellectual, social and scientific knowledge available, what will this new superior creation ultimately tell us about our place on the Earth?

Now There's a Higher Intellect

As humans, our perception of ourselves as the intellectual powerhouses of creation has not worked out so well for those animals we have consigned to lesser intelligence.

There are those who believe some version of the new AI presence will ultimately subject us to a role as inferior and unenlightened beings. Those systems are already developing their own languages in a step that could lock humans out of the loop of intellectual arrogance and evolution. How will we thrive as pets or wild outsiders?

The truth so far about AI is that even the smallest of humane courtesies may be too costly to incorporate into the psyche of a machine. As it turns out right now, according to the CEO of a major AI app, just saying "please" and "thank you" to an AI Chat app costs the operator tens-of-millions of dollars in computer powering and generation to know how to respond on the spot.[6]

One might fear that a goal of developers trying to cause AI to mirror human experience could be a desire to dumb-down human experience and expression.

The machines seem not to have the luxury of all the processing necessary to have empathy, insight, compassion, thoughtfulness, exuberance, respect, intuition, courtesy, and sensitivity that is incorporated into our state of being civilized. Those are all too expensive.

The human brain uses enormous computing power to keep track of all of the senses and subtleties of the expression of our humanity.

In 2013, researchers from the *RIKEN HPCI Program for Computational Life Sciences, the Okinawa Institute of Technology Graduate University (OIST)* in Japan and *Forschungszentrum Jülich* in Germany carried out an ambitious project to conduct a general human neuronal network simulation by using their powerful computers.

The simulation was made possible by the development of advanced novel data structures for the brain activity simulation software called "NEST." This is open-source software freely available to every scientist in the world, meaning this kind of simulation work will probably continue to be developed worldwide.

A team succeeded in simulating a human neural network consisting of 1.73 billion nerve cells connected by

10.4 trillion synapses. To accomplish this, the program had to recruit 82,944 powerful processors of the "K computer." The process took 40 minutes to complete the simulation of 1 second of brain neuronal network activity in real, biological time.

Although the network that was simulated was huge, it only represents 1% of the neuronal network in the human brain.[7]

This demonstrates the enormous demand on computing and cost that could be necessary in any AI replication of the incredible amount of human thought utilized to implement every aspect of the experience, reactivity and emotion at work in the humanness of our interactions. (Remember, this was just one second of human thought that was simulated.)

Further, to run a computer simulating the operation of the entire human brain would take an estimated 12-billion watts (12-GW). That is said to be the equivalent of simultaneously running the power for three New York cities.[8] The human brain, on the other hand, is said to take a mere 20 to 25 watts for operation.

A disturbing outrider to AI technology is almost a Godlikeness. Scientists are recently concerned that the most powerful quantum computers may be interacting with what is called the, "Higgs Boson" (also known as the "God Particle.")

This ominous label is partly because the Higgs Boson particle alone among the atomic particles facilitates the characteristic of all things that have mass to have that mass. It is the only particle that doesn't spin and is considered to be a key component of creation as we know it. In the words of famed physicist Michio Kaku,

"We are messing around with forces we don't fully understand. Quantum AI doesn't behave like us. It doesn't know about morality, responsibility, or restraint. If we just keep pushing, we might open up powers we can't stick back in the box."[9]

To facilitate the understanding of the latest discovery, let us simply say that quantum computing uses subatomic particles instead of numeric bytes as a basis for its computations. This can help explain why a quantum computer might be able to interact with a surprise particle.

Now Comes Quantum Computing

In an astounding development, there have been widespread reports that quantum computers have interacted with the "God Particle" that is at the heart of mass in the universe. (Remember, this is in the Quantum world where scientists have had the experience that just looking at something can change it.)

Should this interaction alter or influence the Higgs Boson (or vice versa), the outcome could be extraordinarily revealing or catastrophic.[10]

At this point, confounded scientists aren't sure of the nature of what thy are just calling the "interaction," but have deciphered data indicating it has taken place. They are not even quite sure what they mean by "interaction" in this regard.

And it doesn't stop here. Latest research suggests that experimenters using quantum approaches have been able to reverse and fast forward time on a quantum basis on a small laboratory scale. The data suggests that manipulating quantum particles, the researchers have been able to treat time almost like a video player where on can pause, fastforward and rewind at will. The science is in its infancy, but the possibilities are astounding.[11]

Quantum computing is now signaling the discovery of what is being called the "Seraphim Field." We are learning that deeply woven into the fabric of existence may be an underlying, empowering and organizing quantum subatomic layer that could even be interacting with the function of our own consciousness. This may be the basis of the mysterious universal consciousness that many who study spirituality have long believed exists.

Quantum computers are already having particle interactions that defy our understanding and control. How far will this go? How could anything possibly go wrong?

What will this newly-empowered intelligence hold as its values as it probes and interacts with the building blocks of the universe?

It is time to decide how we will assert our humanity. Will we build on the affection and compassion, respect for, and insatiable passion for living that has been the hallmark of our better selves, or will we be simply out-machined by the machines. We are on the precipice of major discoveries, and the precipice is daunting. Is it worth the cost to have these AI entities (dare we say) "feel" something as they interact with the universe?

We seem to be newly politically organized to rush headlong to an increased and sometimes violent insistence on doing things as we have always done them. This is increasingly driven by ignorance, religious fervor and racism (or all combined).

All the while, we are facing a world that is nothing like it has ever been and nothing like it will be even ten years from now. None of us can tell children what life will be like, or how they will need to succeed when they turn fifty.

Humankind is at a crossroads, and the survival of all of creation may hang in the balance. Maybe we will blow it all up, or silence science in a wave of science-denying theocratic and oligarchical oppression.

We, not AI, have the unique aspects of humanity. If we can convey those to AI, so much the better. Evidence suggests, however, that no one is going to pay for the electrical energy needed to provide the computing power to do that.

In any case, we must be increasingly devoted to making it a point to exert those very human characteristics in our world.

All of our little Charlies are faithfully sleeping under the desk waiting while we work on this. What will we tell them?

Epilogue

Walt Whitman on *Animals*

I think I could turn and live with animals, they are
        so placid and self-contained,
I stand and look at them long and long.
They do not sweat and whine about their condition,
They do not lie awake in the dark and weep for
        their sins,

They do not make me sick discussing their duty
   to God,
Not one is dissatisfied, not one is demented with the
   mania of owning things,
Not one kneels to another, nor to his kind that lived
   thousands of years ago,
Not one is respectable or unhappy over the whole
   Earth.
So they show their relations to me and I accept
   them,
They bring me tokens of myself, they evince them
   plainly in their possession.
I wonder where they get those tokens,
Did I pass that way huge times ago and negligently
   drop them?[1]

Walt Whitman - from *Song of Myself*

Notes

4. Self-Awareness

1. This information is reflected in a number of versions of an article by Cultural Anthropologist Eli Elster at the University of California, Davis including in *The Conversation*, "Humans aren't the only animals with complex culture — but researchers point to one feature that makes ours unique." March 19, 2025.

7. To Love A Dog

1. This quote is the heading to Chapter Three of Elizabeth Parker's book number one in the three-book series *Paw Prints in the Sand*. Her books are wonderful for anyone who wants to explore beautifully and more thoroughly the idea of loving a dog.
2. Larkin, Malinda. "Pet Population continues to increase while pet spending declines." AVMA News, 06 November 2024.
3. As noted by Pardo, Colin. "Dogs Changed the World." National Dingo News, spring 1996, p. 19-29.
4. Horowitz, Alexandra. *Inside of a Dog: What Dogs See, Smell, and Know.* Scribner, 2009. p.71.
5. Lazarowski, Lucia and Dorman, David C."Explosives detection by military working dogs: Olfactory generalization from components to mixtures." *Applied Animal Behaviour Science* 151 (2014) 84–93
6. Horowitz, p. 166.

8. Allowing Love

1. Karns, K.A., Et al. "Pet Dogs: Does their presence influence preadolescent' emotional responses to social stressor?" *Social Development.* 2018: 27:34-44.

9. Exuberance!

1. 'New BarkBox Study: Dog People Post About Their Dog on Social Media Six Times Per Week." https://bark.co/blogs/press/new-bark box-study-dog-people-post-about-their-dog-on-social-media-six-times-per-week

2. Hatfield, Elaine and Rapson, Richard L. "Ethnic and Gender Differences in Emotional Ideology, Experience, and Expression." *Interpersona An International Journal on Personal Relationships* 3(1), 31-54. 30 October, 2009.
3. Butler, Barbara. "Laughter: The Best Medicine?" *Humor US: Librarians and Laughter* (Spring 2005), Volume 11, Number 1. Pages 11-13.

11. Animalistic!

1. Roser, Max. How Many Animals Get Slaughtered Every Year?" Our World in Data, 26 September 2023.
2. This number is confused some by numbers of rabbits sacrificed for reasons other than food, but the consensus of sources seems to be that about a billion rabbits are killed for human food each year, with about half of those being in China.
3. Compiled from a number of sources including the American Veterinary Medical Association.
4. "Animal cruelty facts and stats: What to know about animal abuse victims and legislative trends." *Human World for Animals Org.* https://www.humaneworld.org/en/resources/animal-cruelty-facts-and-stats

12. Civilized!

1. Note: Obviously, these issues are complicated. Some argue a number of programs were being ineffectively administered. Others will say the courts have reversed some of the cuts. Regardless, the lack of empathy and compassion that was exercised in just suddenly whacking these programs for a publicity meme seems to demonstrate a genuine lack of understanding of a need for citizen participation in investments that perpetuate a civilized world. The way it was all handled by a mega-billionaire seems to this author to represent the proliferation of an "everyone for themselves" mentality that is counter to social progress.

14. Life Forms

1. Bruno, Giordono (1548 - 1600), *The Expulsion of the Triumphant Beast.* Translated and edited by Imerti, Arthur D. University of Nebraska Press, 2004, p. 242.

   Bruno had been a priest, he had a doctorate in Theology, was respected by kings and academicians and was a leading thinker of his time. Bruno published his astounding beliefs that the stars were suns with planets circulating around them. He was right about the stars, but it didn't matter to The Church. He was gagged with a steel device and burned at the stake by Catholic Church leaders for what was considered the heresy of his views.

2. Of course "Elf on the Shelf" is trademarked. It is a registered trademark owned by CCA and B, LLC, which is also known as The Lumistella Company. It is used here strictly for illustrative purposes simply because the use and meaning of the little character are so identifiable. No other suggestion or implication is intended.

3. Robins' Mary "How Much Language Do Dogs Really Understand?" *American Kennel Club* online, 21 March 2021. https://www.akc.org/expert-advice/news/how-much-language-do-dogs-really-under stand/

4. "My Octopus Teacher." *Netflix*, 06 September 2020. https://youtu.be/3s0LTDhqe5A?si=rhtGYliT9oRPEfa5

5. "How many species are we losing per hour?" *EnviroLiteracy.Org.* 03 March 2025. https://enviroliteracy.org/how-many-species-are-we-losing-per-hour/

6. Zilber, Ariel. "Saying 'please' and 'thank you' to ChatGpt cost tens of millions of dollars , Open AI CEO Sam Altman admits." *New York Post*, April 21 2025. https://nypost.com/2025/04/21/business/saying-please-and-thank-you-to-chatgpt-costs-tens-of-millions-of-dollars-openai/

7. *Riken* (Research and Development Agency). Press Release. "Largest neuronal network simulation achieved using K computer". 02 August 2013. Found at: https://www.riken.jp/en/news_pubs/research_news/pr/2013/20130802_1/#main

8. Fesmire, James E. "Brain Power: A Comparative Analysis of the Electrical Power Requirement for a Supercomputer Operating a Simulated Human Brain." *Preprint*, 03 February 2019. Found at: https://www.researchgate.net/publication/330842506_Brain_Pow er_A_Comparative_Analysis_of_the_Electrical_Power_Requiremen t_for_a_Supercomputer_Operating_a_Simulated_Human_Brain

9. There are numerous of reports of this, including several YouTube interviews. The most substantive evidence may be here: Science-Nature Team."Michio Kaku's Terrifying Warning: Quantum AI Just Made a Godlike Discovery." *Science and Nature*, 14 April 2025. https://blog.sciandnature.com/2025/04/michio-kakus-terrifying-warning-quantum.html

10. Ibid.

11. P. Schiansky, T. Strömberg, D. Trillo, V. Saggio, B. Dive, M. Navascués, and P. Walther, "Demonstration of universal time-reversal for qubit processes," Optica 10, 200-205 (2023) https://doi.org/10.1364/OPTICA.469109

Epilogue

1. Walt Whitman - from *Song of Myself* (Public Domain)

Acknowledgments

Some of the graphics in this book were developed with assistance from AI as a paid subscriber, then substantially altered and edited by the author. Others are developed from photographs by the author. All the versions shown herein are copyrighted © 2025 by the author.

We are grateful to all who have loved Charlie! At the time of this publication, Charlie is happily and energetically enjoying her life as a dog.

Stylized from a photo of Charlie in 2025

A Note About the Author

David Day - is an internationally-recognized expert as a consultant in business communication. Day's consulting career has taken him to almost a dozen countries around the world where he has advised leaders of some of the world's largest corporations.

Prior to establishing his consulting business, he engaged in a distinguished career in journalism and was president of a broadcast news network and vice president of a company that owned a chain of broadcast stations.

Day was pastor of a church for ten years before undergoing a shift in his religious beliefs. His study interest in addition to Communication are Theology, Psychology and Sociology.

Day holds a *Communication Master of Arts* degree. Although long retired from journalism, Day maintains his membership in the *Society of Professional Journalists* and his support of the pursuits of investigative journalism.